SPRINGBANK PAPERS

Through the Sun's Eyes
Volume 2

Jim Conlon

Springbank Papers
Through the Sun's Eyes
Volume 2

By Jim Conlon

©2022 Jim Conlon

Published by:
Nicasio Press
Sebastopol, California

All rights reserved. No part of this publication may be reproduced, stored in a retrieval system, or transmitted in any form or by any means (electronic, mechanical, photocopying, recording, or otherwise) without the prior written permission of the author and the publisher.

ISBN: 978-1-7375814-4-4

Dedication

To all who have made Springbank what it is.

Table of Contents

Prologue 3
Springbank Retreat 4
Searching 7
The Journey 8
Discovering Mystery 9
Springbank Is a Verb 10
At Mepkin Abbey 13
A Monastic Journey 14
Sacred Moment 16
Morning at Mepkin 17
Wisdom Figures 18
Thomas Merton 21
Energy 24
Blessed Day 26
St. Bernard 27
In Silence 29
Longing of the Heart 30
Where is God? 31
Prayers for New Beginnings 32
As Yet To Be 34
Transitions 35
Toward Theopoetics 36
Amplify 37
Vital and Amazed 38
The Future of the Church 39
Contemplative Thoughts 41
The Emergence of Integral Ecology 42
The Fourfold Wisdom of Thomas Berry 43
Reflections on the New Story 44
Re-sacrilization 45
An Invitation 46

Our Way Into the Future	47
Present Moment	48
Many Wells, One River	49
Celebrating Indigenous Peoples' Day	50
Lily of the Mohawks	51
Toward a Creation-Centered Civilization	52
Pastel People	55
Listen	56
Stunning	57
Insurrection	58
A New Epoch	59
Mystical Moment	60
From the Womb of Wonder	62
Tomorrow	63
Thanksgiving 2021	64
Let's Pray	66
Thanksgiving Prayer	67
Christmas Prayer	68
Family Prayer	69
Prayer of the Cosmos	70
Whatever Needs to Be Done	74
The Exultet for Today's World: Easter Vigil 2021	76
Solitude and Dark	79
Conscious Fear, Unconscious Wish	80
Where Were You on 9/11?	81
Death	82
Descent	83
The Other Side	84
How Do You Pray?	86
Earth	88
Plans	89
Our Great Work	90
Women's Wisdom	91

Sacred Water	92
Unfinished	94
Our Broken Story	95
How the Scientific Story Becomes a Sacred Story	96
Sacred Heart Church in Port Lambton, 2017	98
Better Than the Past	101
The Challenge Before Us Now	102
Birth of a New Soul	104
Each Day	105
Matthew Fox: Early Years	106
Matthew Fox and Fr. Chenu	107
Matthew Fox: Creation Spirituality	108
Don't Shrink	110
The Four Paths: *Via Positiva*	111
The Four Paths: *Via Negativa*	112
Our Vision Realized	114
Next Teardrop	115
The Four Paths: *Via Creativa*	116
Creativity	117
The Four Paths: *Via Transformativa*	118
Only Now	120
Questions	121
Imagine a World	122
Getting Started	123
Welcome	124
The Radiance of Springbank	125
Epilogue: Concluding Prayer	127
About the Author	129

Springbank Papers

Through the Sun's Eyes

SPRINGBANK PAPERS

Prologue

In this second volume of *Springbank Papers*, I invite all members of the Springbank community to continue to join me on the journey of my life.

It has been a journey of pastoral ministry, community organization, urban training, communication therapy, creation spirituality, the new cosmology, geo-justice and engaged cosmology, poetry, and other modes of understanding.

This journey has brought me to Springbank Retreat, where my soul has found an abiding home.

Springbank Retreat

Springbank Retreat is a radiant, sacred place.
Everywhere there is beauty—
on the pin oak trees that mark the cosmic story,
and on the white stone gate that welcomes
both the seeker and the sacred.

Springbank is a healing place
where beauty soothes the soul,
a place that welcomes all,
who come from near and far,
seeking its refuge.

Springbank is a home
for Max, Jake and Shelly,
and for all who seek and sow
stories that reveal our deepest longings
and the wonder of each soul.

Springbank is a place to pray,
to see the divine
in every drop of rain that falls,
to dive into the great unknown
and discover what life is all about.

Yes, Springbank is a place of rest
for each eager soul,
a place to discover a new tomorrow.
Because there is no turning back,
only a surprising new tomorrow.

Jim Conlon

Springbank is a place of trust and hope,
a silent stairway to the cosmos,
a place to walk the cosmic path,
to be conscious and aware of divine love
and discover what you have always sought.

Springbank is a place
of sacred beauty, both fragile and strong,
where out of seeming nothingness,
a silent hunch appears,
announcing the future that unfolds up ahead.

More than anything,
Springbank is a place to just be,
surrounded by each moment, fresh and new,
to knit up the ragged sleeve of care
and come home to what is next.

Yes, Springbank is a place
where tomorrow billows forth,
where stories are told
and discovery happens,
where seekers come home to God.

Searching

Sacred seeker, look backward.
Find a new perspective on what was
and on what comes tumbling
back again today.

Is this not a time
to reinvent your life,
to see the wisdom
of what is now past?

Honor with gratitude
the days that lie ahead.
Pray without ceasing
for what is yet to come.

The Journey

When the long night is over,
may your soul come to rest
in the days that remain.
May your listening heart
be embraced by holy mystery.

When the long day is over,
may we celebrate the dusk,
welcome the night,
then rise at dawn
to continue the quest.

JIM CONLON

Discovering Mystery

I went down into my inmost self.
As I descended deeper and deeper,
I began to lose contact with myself.
What emerged I do not know.

As I continued to descend,
I went beyond any division within myself.
The descent took me
to a place beyond all two-ness.

Out of this dissolving emergence,
I began to discover beyondness.
I became aware of a well-spring
I dare to call my life.

Springbank Is a Verb

Springbank is a sacred place
where the great work is done,
a place of strong beginnings,
where imaginations soar
and creative works unfold.
A place where reinvention happens
and humanity becomes new again.

Yes, Springbank is a verb,
through which we move into action
and leave what's lost behind.
Springbank is a place
where we renew ourselves
through memory and reflection.
Springbank is a place to grow our soul
in the garden of our great work.

At Mepkin Abbey

On June 14, 2021, I ventured forth to Mepkin Abbey in Moncks Corner, South Carolina. My plan was to join the monastic community for the summer months. I remained there until September 17.

I am grateful to Trina McCormick for arranging with Superior Fr. Joe and his community to welcome me to the Abbey.

When I arrived, I began to settle into the rhythm of the days. It took some time to adjust to the dynamics of monastic life.

Mepkin Abbey embraces the rule of St. Benedict, which was composed and practiced in the early church. His vision was based on an integration of prayer and work. He said, "To pray is to work, and to work is to pray."

Based on this balanced approach to life, the monks spend each day at work. This can include writing, preparing the liturgical programs, kitchen work, caring for the infirm, providing spiritual companionship to community members and visitors, administrative work, and responses to whatever needs to be done.

The gift of monastic living is clarity. The gift of peace that emerges illuminates the soul and makes more accessible the sacredness of everyday existence.

My Mepkin experience was an affirmation of the kinds of challenges, joys, and sorrows that continue to have an impact on all of our lives.

A Monastic Journey

At Mepkin Abbey, the monastic schedule may seem out of step with the dominant culture but it provides a way to God, in and through silence, memory, and anticipation. Out of the deep well of solitude, participants gain access to holy mystery, to what remains hidden in soft ripples of tranquility.

Each monk at Mepkin greets the morning with matins and lauds. Each day, the community gathers for a Eucharistic celebration at 7:30 a.m. On Sunday, the Eucharist is at 10 a.m. and is often attended by outside visitors.

The daily schedule continues through seven intervals of prayer. Periodically throughout the day, the bell rings and invites people to prayer.

During the main meal at noon, a reading from a chosen book is offered to the community. While I was in residence, we read from the writings of Pope Francis, which urge us to dream. These teachings were keenly felt, as we were immersed in the pandemic that has ravaged so many lives.

Each day at the Abbey culminates at 8 p.m. with compline, the evening prayer. This is followed by each member of the community walking in front of Fr. Joe and receiving a sprinkling with holy water as they go off to their rooms for the night.

The schedule is different on Fridays, which is called *desert day*. This term came from the vision and practice of Charles de Foucauld, the founder of the Desert Fathers. The focus of the desert day schedule is on personal prayer. The day closes with a benediction with the blessed sacrament, as the community sings together the Salve Regina.

Each night, when I went to bed at 8 p.m. in room no. 8, I was plunged into memories of my seminary days.

Sacred Moment

Breathe softly into the solitude.
Allow silence to be your friend.
Out of darkness, a beam of light appears.
Each sacred moment dissolves into beauty
and awakens childhood memories of Earth.
Each newfound experience reveals a clarity
that arises from within
and washes across your open, grateful heart.

Jim Conlon

Morning at Mepkin

The bell rings announcing this day.
We gather in the chapel to pray.
We say hello to the flowers and the rain.
We welcome the day
and give thanks for all that has been
and for all that will be.

As each morning I venture
across the fields of Mepkin Abbey,
I once again begin the monastic journey
to work and pray
in response to the promptings
of St. Benedict's rule.

I invite each of you
to give thanks to the great spirit
who brought you to where you are,
to reflect on the defining moments
of your personal journey.

May each of our lives
respond to the sacred impulse
and holy mystery that prompted
our presence here today.
Amen.

Wisdom Figures

Two of the wisdom figures in our Springbank story are Thomas Merton and Thomas Berry. Each of these prophetic voices provides an enduring vision as we look to the future.

My experience at Mepkin Abbey reactivated my interest in the work, words, and life of Thomas Merton.

Merton was a man of both vision and practice. One could describe his life and his wisdom as the search for the true self. He understood the presence of the invisible divine, which we can neither feel, touch, nor smell. Nevertheless, we understand that the divine is fully present in everything we can feel, touch, or smell.

His work and words flow from the rich, florescent wisdom of all creation, which permeates all things.

Merton was a poet, photographer, and writer. He had an appreciation for painting, music, dance, and pottery. He is the author of some sixty books covering a wide spectrum of insight and interest. Today, more than forty years since his untimely death by electrocution in a shower in Bangkok, it is almost impossible to enter any bookstore and not see at least one copy of his books. You will find copies of his works at Springbank.

Credit: https://thomasmerton.org/

Thomas Merton

In the early 1960s, before Vatican II, a book rested comfortably on the bookshelf in my room in the seminary. Today that book is yellowed with age. The title of the book is *Seeds of Contemplation*. Its author is Thomas Merton. From that moment until today, I have had an enduring fascination with Merton and his written works.

When Pope Francis visited the United States, he mentioned Thomas Merton—along with Abraham Lincoln, Dorothy Day, and Dr. Martin Luther King, Jr.—as an outstanding example of significant people in the American church.

Merton was a child of the universe. In his journey, he awakened to the realization that life is replete with wonder and surprise.

Merton was born in France. His father was from New Zealand, and his mother was from the United States. His mother died when he was five years old, and his father died when he was a teenager. Both of his parents were artists.

Merton's early years in England were marked by a time when, as the expression goes, he "sowed his wild oats." Later, he was brought to the United States to live under the supervision of a grandparent.

During his graduate work at Columbia University, Merton composed a final paper on the writings of William Blake. He worked for a period of time in Harlem with Catherine Doherty and was deeply moved by her work.

While living in the Black community of Harlem, he was drawn to the love of the people and felt called to the monastic life. He felt seized by an amazing openness. He was raised as an Anglican yet felt called to become a Catholic. He was received into the church at a local parish in New York City. Later, he applied to join the Franciscan community. His request was denied when it became known that he had fathered a child during his early years.

Merton was able to follow the longings of his heart, which led him through much searching and ultimately to the Trappist monastery Our Lady of Gethsemane, in Bardstown, Kentucky, near the city of Louisville. There he discovered his vocation and decided to become a monk, a priest, and a writer. In 1941, he was accepted into the monastery.

One day in Louisville, he suddenly was freed from the dream of separateness. At the corner of Fourth and Walnut, he was moved by the realization that he loved everybody.

Candidates flocked to Gethsemane. Merton was responsible for a monastic renaissance. As his life unfolded, so did his writings. With the encouragement of his abbot, he composed an autobiography of his life as a monk. The title of this book is *The Seven Storey Mountain*. Remarkably, his book became a bestseller. Through it, he became well known.

Soon after that, his book *New Seeds of Contemplation* was published. His work continued to reach wide audiences. His books include *The Sign of Jonas* and *Conjectures of a Guilty Bystander* and as many as sixty or more other titles.

While on retreat at Mepkin Abbey in the summer of 2021, I took into my hands a copy of *The Sign of Jonas*. This book contains the story of Merton's journey through his years of preparation for the ministry, and it also corresponds to the events of our present day. During my time at the abbey, I felt the prophetic vision of Thomas Merton present on every page.

While Merton's early writings reflected the separation of a monk from the world, the focus of his later writings shifted to issues of the world. He began to address topics of war and peace, nuclear war, civil rights and race, sensitivity to the natural world, the beauty of creation, and many other themes. As a result, his body of work placed him as one of the significant writers of his time. His writings and memorabilia are housed today at Bellarmine College.

Once, when Merton was concerned about some of the issues of his life at Gethsemane, a friend suggested that an option might be for him to leave. His response was profound and moving: "Yes, but you don't understand, this is my home."

It is my hope and prayer that we become familiar with the wisdom and mission of Thomas Merton's life. May we as Springbank people, regardless of geography, culture, or origin, take to heart his words. May we be inspired to live a life filled with spiritual practice and treasured moments of silence, solitude, prayer, and contemplation.

Energy

Energy is swirling,
churning into spiral paths,
flowing from memories of struggle,
waiting and watching,
yearning for fresh moments,
culminating moments.

Memories cascade
into the present moment.
Past struggles are surprised
as a new time appears,
a liberating time
of recollection, love, and letting go.

Jim Conlon

Blessed Day

We came from the ocean,
that vast sacred place
where dreams are enacted
and great stories told.

As we await our arrival,
the great gift from on high,
may we bless each new moment
on this Springbank day.

Undefended and open,
each soul gently waits.
May this day be blessed
and burst forth with gratitude.

St. Bernard

Thomas Merton's view of life was profoundly influenced by the writings of St. Bernard of Clairvaux, who encouraged people to embrace the beauty of the natural world.

St. Bernard is well known for his view that the divine is a revelatory presence in creation. He proclaimed his conviction with these words: "You will find something more in woods than in books. Trees and stones will teach you that which you can never learn from masters." He believed that our encounter with creation can be a revelatory experience.

For Merton, nature was the primary source of revelation that permeates and infuses every part of creation.

Sr. Miriam of Genesis Farm named comprehension of this experience *earth literacy*. Through earth literacy, we are able to express and confirm that there are in fact two scriptures: the book of the Bible and the book of creation. These represent two ways we can access divine revelation.

In Silence

Thomas Berry said, "In silence, God ceases to be an object and becomes an experience."

During my days at Mepkin Abbey, I began to understand the intent of those words. One of the great gifts of silence and solitude was to experience a dissolution of the pre-occupations that arise in response to a busy imagination and mind.

As members of the monastic community, we would pray, "I'm listening. But I don't know if what I hear is silence or God."

To achieve clarity of consciousness, the monk transcends the distractions by becoming absorbed in the silence of everyday life.

When I experienced the grand silence each evening at Mepkin, my awareness plunged into an envelope of solitude and darkness.

Often I would venture to the shores of the Cooper River. There I felt awash in the beauty of the river, the fish, the boats.

In each moment of solitude and silence, I felt a fresh energy and the holy mystery revealed. I experienced a wake-up call that reminded me of friendships and commitments that call out for courage as well as gratitude. An appreciation for creativity bubbled up out of the deep wells of solitude.

Today I give great thanks for the elevated awareness that comes to us in solitude, as we gain access to each sacred monastic moment.

Longing of the Heart

In the monastic experience, we can respond to the longing in our hearts that speaks to us from the edge of wonder. That longing calls us to respond to what the divine is offering.

Thomas Merton experienced this longing. He wrote, "If I never become what I am meant to be, but always remain what I am not, I shall spend eternity contradicting myself by being at once something and nothing."

At Mepkin Abbey, at the cusp of new beginnings, I felt liberated from the static guidance of the past and anticipated a compassionate future.

I experienced a clarity and wisdom manifest in each revelatory moment that nourished the vast meanderings of my mind.

Jim Conlon

Where is God?

Where is God in the midst of pain?
That place where I cannot see,
where I dissolve
into a crumbling pile of nothing,
where awareness fades,
where nothing seems stable and alive.

Then out of apparent nothingness and terror,
I perceive rising before me
a cosmic moment that embraces every joy,
every jagged edge of life.

Somehow, even amidst pain,
imbalance and embarrassment,
I discover comfort and rest,
a place that exists despite my uncertainty.
A fresh spring flows out of a vast emptiness.
This spring is the wellspring of my life.

At this moment, I celebrate
and give thanks for the cosmic embrace
of the divine mystery,
so replete with terror and love.

Prayers for New Beginnings

At the precipice
of new beginnings,
I sit back and sink
into each conscious moment.
With a heart broken open
to the beauty and brokenness of life,
I perceive the heartfelt wisdom
I want to anticipate
and meet tomorrow.

As Yet To Be

Beauty shines forth
as each listening heart
nourishes and blesses
a thirsting soul.

In this defining moment,
everywhere you look,
radiant energy flows
across each wounded heart.

An all-inclusive vision
flows across the sky
and comes to rest
in silent peace.

A spring of solitude
feeds the flow of radiant energy,
making possible
what is yet to be.

Transitions

Transitions are awesome moments. In them, we let go into a great abyss, our destiny unknown.

Transitions invite us to plunge into rivers of grace. Out of loss and emptiness, a vision emerges. An upstart spring bursts forth and flows on.

All who loved and knew you, James Joseph, will miss you. You are a friend of God and of artists. Your rendition of "Danny Boy" breaks open all our Celtic hearts. Your sudden transition left us saddened and surprised, wondering at the mystery of it all.

Today we hear again your voice, remember your family and your many friends, through whom your spirit gave us life.

Today we pray.

May your present life be better than all the past. Today is a time of great expectation, a time of wondering when the great spirit will descend upon us. A time of waiting to arrive, to be present, to come home to ourselves, to celebrate the sacred moment.

Toward Theopoetics

In the 1970s, Stanley Hopper coined the term *theopoetics*. He was talking about the power of language to guide our understanding of God.

Similarly, Thomas Berry once advised us that when the path ahead appears unclear, the best thing we might do is to write a poem.

From this perspective, we plunge into the waiting arms of the great spirit and once again become immersed in an ocean of grace. Our awareness dissolves any hint of alienation or separation. Immersed in this sacred space, we embrace creativity, and our spirit soars beyond conscious thought. In this revelatory moment, we are able to discover the divine within our lived experience of creativity.

Such moments can be understood as a breaking in upon the world that takes us by surprise. We use words to take us beyond conscious thought and into spiritual awakening. These words empower us to peer into the future—a glorious future, a vision that speaks of fresh possibilities for life and for engaging with our authentic true self.

Amplify

Consciousness makes it possible
for us to reflect on our awareness.
Each person receives the gift of reflection.
In so doing, we amplify our imagination,
impulse and intuition.

Vital and Amazed

Today we celebrate
the gifts of our cousin and kin,
all who walk on Earth,
fly through the air,
swim in the oceans.
We celebrate those
who cleanse, purify and protect
the oceans of grace,
as we embark
on the journey of beauty
that is revealed
to each vital and amazing soul.

The Future of the Church

Today I stop and hope to pray
with thanks for all I have received.
I offer friendship, trust and gratitude
to the Cosmic One,
who is present everywhere.
I pray for my heart,
for my soul,
for God in all things.
His creative energy and love
permeate all that is.
From this place,
the future of the church is born.

Contemplative Thoughts

Here on the Palmetto meadow stands a legacy of faith, a monastic community that celebrates the contemplative life.

I call out into the silence of the night, waiting, hoping, praying into the darkness that surrounds me. From this place, I send out echoes of silence, while I continue to wonder what all this means.

With each passing day, I am puzzled and wonder what's next. Surrounded by solitude and silence, I wonder about the meaning of life.

What are the remaining chapters in my as-yet-unlived life?

I pray and listen and ask, "What is it all about? Am I talking to God or simply to myself?"

The Emergence of Integral Ecology

Thomas Berry, Teilhard de Chardin, and Leonardo Boff were aware that after two world wars, the sense of spiritual energy in the Western world was significantly diminished. Teilhard called out that what the believing community needed was a fresh energy and zest for life.

Throughout history, the Catholic community, especially through the ministry of religious women, has been devoted to the poor and the oppressed. However, the same was not true regarding ecology and care of the Earth.

Then, through the publication of *Laudato Si'*, Pope Francis proposed a dynamic integration between social justice and ecological resurgence.

For the first time, the Catholic community, under the leadership of Pope Francis and many collaborators, achieved a new understanding, which is signified in the encyclical *Laudato Si'*.

The Fourfold Wisdom of Thomas Berry

Thomas Berry shared his understanding of the great work: "History is governed by those overarching movements that give shape and meaning to life by relating the human venture to the large destinies of the universe."

These days, we may be entering the new time of hope Thomas Berry referred to as the era of the fourfold wisdom. This wisdom provides us with the opportunity to create an inclusive human presence that opens us to the ultimate mystery that resides at the heart of the universe.

The fourfold wisdom is as follows:
- The wisdom of women, who offer the gift of radical inclusiveness
- The wisdom of Indigenous people, who participate in the functioning of the natural world and celebrate the presence of divinity in many manifestations
- The wisdom of classical traditions, based on revelatory experience both immanent and transcendent (wisdom in the West is understood as Islam, Judaism, and Christianity; in the East as Hinduism, Buddhism, Confucianism, and others)
- The wisdom of science, which has become the foundation for our sacred story, making possible a more mutually enhancing world

As these wisdoms come together and converge, we gain an enhanced sense of the sacred and evoke the great work of the universe itself.

Reflections on the New Story

The new story is not so much an idea as it is a numinous experience, an experience prompted by the holy mystery of the universe.

It calls us into an experience of intimacy, awe, and wonder.

The new story was born out of the imagination of Teilhard de Chardin and Thomas Berry. This awesome journey, this universe story, reveals its beginnings through the great flaring forth. It reveals where we are now and provides a glimpse of the future.

It is a story that calls us forth into life, to empower us to heal what is broken and to renew, beautify, and invigorate the planet and its people.

The universe story is not a book or a collection of rational thoughts. Rather, it is an encounter with holy mystery, a profound awareness of being enveloped in beauty and wonder.

In this way, the universe itself becomes the context for all the next events in our lives.

We set out to heal the split and the dualism that separate the divine from all creation.

Re-sacrilization

The new story is
a celebration
of the re-sacralization of Earth.
It signals a time
to heal all separation
and to inaugurate a new future
for the believing community.
We can say
the new story is
an opportunity
to return to our origins.

An Invitation

Today we are invited to fall in love with Earth and all creation.

We are invited to recover in each of our souls the zeal, passion, and purpose that are present and available to us in the primary sacrament, which is Earth and all creation.

We are invited to invoke and celebrate a love affair with all creation.

One of Thomas Berry's important insights is that the theology of the past has been afflicted with too much transcendence. By that, he meant that there was a deep, dualistic wound in the experience of the believing community.

Although he did not use the term, the panentheism of the eighteenth century emphasized that God is in all things (immanence).

Berry invites us to spend more time on creation and less time on redemption.

We are invited to understand through this healing process that each of our stories is a paragraph in the great story. God didn't just plunk us here.

One of the great contributions of Thomas Berry is that he gave spiritual significance to the scientific evidence of evolution. Having woven this integration into a seamless garment, he invites us to become aware of our story as a sacred story.

Our Way Into the Future

To understand the science of evolution as the source of an evolutionary faith that is sacred, Thomas Berry said that three dynamic principles are operative in all of life. For these principles, there is no equation but rather the affirmation of lived experience.

These are:
- Nothing in the universe is the same; there are no two things alike. We call this principle *differentiation*.
- It is also true that, not only are things different, but they are all interconnected. The cosmological term for this is *communion*.
- Finally, each expression of creation has a life principle, a subjectivity, Thomas called *interiority*. This principle is present in all of life from the very beginning.

As we reflect on these principles, we begin to understand that through the transmission of these values, the scientific story of the universe becomes a sacred story.

Present Moment

At this present moment,
all previous memories dissolve,
vanish and disappear.
You now know,
it seems for the first time,
the experience of the beyondness.

Without a name,
a deep sense of wisdom
bubbles up from within.
The holy mystery,
that emerging presence,
remains distant yet all embracing.

It is the mystery you have spent your days pursuing.
It is the pulse of life that sometimes happens
when you return to a place you have been before
and rest in the joyful embrace
of the one you always knew.
Yet for the first time, you feel prompted
to consciously celebrate and give thanks.

Many Wells, One River

There is a joy in my heart,
a slow harmony
that brings everything together,
an amazing radiant energy
that flows into each surprising moment,
that heals all things together
to make our world one.

All our unique expressions
are woven together.
Yes, each unique expression,
however distinct,
is woven with all the others.
We may be many wells,
but we all become one river.

Celebrating Indigenous Peoples' Day

At Springbank and other communities around America, we join First Nations people to celebrate and honor Indigenous Peoples' Day.

This is a sacred day. We join our voices in thanksgiving to celebrate the fruits of Earth that nourish our souls and strengthen our bodies.

On this memorable day, we remember and give thanks for the living legacy of ancestral grace that preceded us on the Indigenous journey. Among those we honor are Black Elk, Chief Seattle, Buck Ghost Horse, Sister Jose Hobday, as well as our own Indigenous roots. In their names and in reverence for this sacred land, we gather today around the Grandmother Tree.

We give thanks for the spiritual practices that our Indigenous ancestors celebrated here among the trees. Among the gifts of Indigenous wisdom are respect for silence, gratitude for the sacredness of land, the prayer lodge, and the spirit quest.

With Thomas Berry, we celebrate this sacred Indigenous day as we reflect on his words: "We never experienced this land as they did—as a living presence not primarily to be used but to be revered and communed with."

Lily of the Mohawks

Remember and give thanks today
for the life of the first Indigenous soul
canonized here in America.
St. Kateri was infected with smallpox as a child.
Her sight was impaired,
and as a native person,
she bore the burden of oppression
because of her brown skin.

She was baptized at the age of 19
and died when she was 23.
Because of her diminished vision,
she was named Kateri,
the one who groped her way.
Her parting words were
"I am not my own."

These days are marked by revelations.
The bodies of many Indigenous children
discovered in unmarked graves
in British Columbia and elsewhere in Canada.
Today let us pray that the revelation
of this tragedy will bring forth
enhanced justice and peace
for First Nations people.

Toward a Creation-Centered Civilization

Moved by an urgency to understand my experience and yours, I am reminded of the pervasive influence of the dominant culture. I come to you to celebrate instead a creation-centered tradition.

Our intention is to build a new global civilization. This will lead to a palpable pulsation, a new at-homeness in the creation tradition that is authentic and shareable in our time.

Let us look at society more critically today. Let us move beyond simple cooperation and explore a process that reflects the perspective of the oppressed, the marginalized, the voiceless.

We look toward a creation-centered theology and are encouraged to explore this truly refreshing avenue, which will enable us to grow our engagement in life.

This prophetic work can heal the cosmic aneurisms and energize our movement toward a symphony of beauty and wonder that is both daring and prophetic.

Yes, we are invited into a universe where the human and the divine are united, where a new civilization can be born.

We are moved today by a vision that is nourished by the sacred dimensions of Earth. It is a vision of the kind of world we would like to build. We approach this process, in which blessing, letting go, creativity, and compassion are revealed

We live in a time when some elements of society are experiencing a deep spiritual awakening. This awakening offers us the opportunity to become more engaged in our ever-deepening spiritual journey. It is a journey that sees life as fluid, oceanic, and deeply creative.

We need each other to name our journey and create our future. It is an approach that can lead to personal and social transformation, and it is being kept alive by the artists, painters, potters, and prophets.

I grew up near a Native American reservation and was fascinated with their lifestyle, ministry, and religion. I was impressed by their music, dance, and ritual. I became more and more interested in the tragedy and triumph of Indigenous souls as I reflected on Wounded Knee and the profound respect Native American people carry for the rhythm of the seasons and for the Creator and Earth.

Today we ask for a vision, for increased awareness, for hope, and for an energizing future. May this vision energize us as we each search for our soul.

Yes, it is time for civilization to enter a new era. The creation-centered tradition must move from the psyche to the social structures. Our dreams for a global civilization can be visioned, practiced, and made new.

Together we gather to name a vision for the new creation-centered civilization that is not yet but is about to be born.

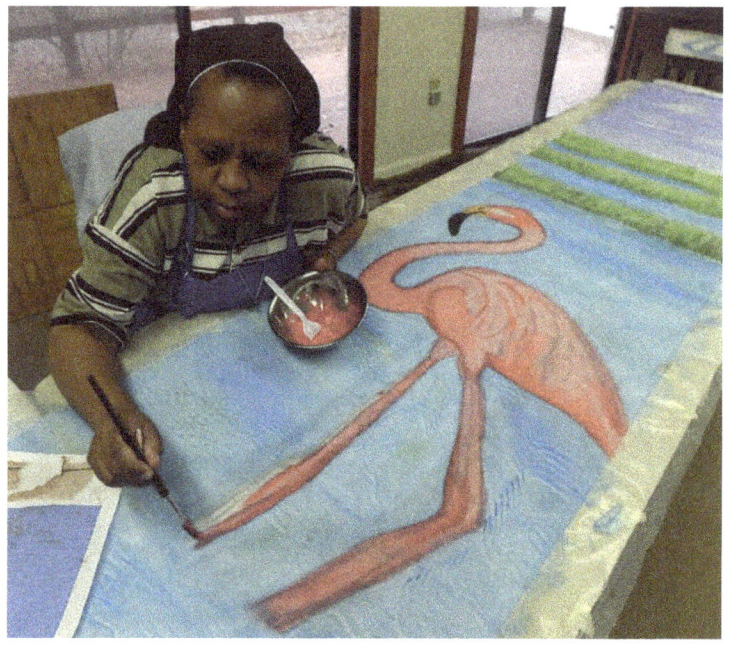

Jim Conlon

Pastel People

Brush, water and paint.
Colors portray the fire:
the fire in the universe,
the fire burning in the forest,
the fire in my heart.

Go to the edges,
then paint the center of the paper.
And your life.
Pastels balance intensity and solitude.
Let the Earth speak.

Bring back the awe and wonder of it all.
Color me red, yellow and blue.
Make me a picture.
Flow into the pigment
you call your life.

Listen

Listen to the promptings.
Experience expectation.
You will find what you seek.

Don't rush after it.
It was there all the time.
Rest in this soft awareness.

The sacred one is at your side.
Speak softly from your soul.
Listen from this hidden place.

Stunning

Allow the joy of life
to flow across your soul.
Each pulsating moment
breaks through
across a vast panorama,
as the endless sky
causes you to shiver
at a profound beauty
too stunning to behold.

Insurrection

Today marks the moment
when a plan to overthrow
our system of government
was unleashed.
The insurrection was
an attempt to annihilate democracy.
As we reflect on this event,
we are confronted with questions:
What are our defining moments?
What should we as a believing community explore?
How should we respond?
Today we are asked,
"What am I on this Earth to accomplish?"

A New Epoch

Over the years, I have reflected on cultural epochs as identifiable benchmarks in the course of history. A new epoch awaits us that is as yet unclear.

This new epoch has many names. It is the search for wisdom, for a numinous future, for evoking an image of the not-yet. Some wisdom figures have used names like the ecological age and ecozoic era to capture the sense of a positive future, hoped for but not yet realized.

We are inspired by courageous acts of hope that hold promise for the unfolding future.

What is needed today is participation in a decisive and spontaneous burst of energy that is infused with the power of the human heart and the support of friends and colleagues. What is needed is a transformed consciousness with which to meet the new ecological age.

Mystical Moment

One of the most enduring moments during my recent stay at Mepkin Abbey was inspired by silence and solitude. Something happened in my soul. It was as if out of nothingness a clarity of consciousness emerged.

It was an experience I had previously been unable to achieve either through therapy or meditation. My preoccupation with worry vanished, like a cloud dissolving. In its place, clarity emerged. My heart felt infused with aliveness. Gratitude and aliveness bubbled up.

It was a mystical moment, overflowing with a radiant gift from the universe that I can only name as silence or God.

Jim Conlon

From the Womb of Wonder

Born from the sacred womb
of solitude and silence,
from the womb of wonder,
expressions of sadness and joy
bring a message,
call out into emptiness
with a resounding prayer of wonder.

Tomorrow

What lies up ahead?
Is it darkness, uncertainty and doubt
or an unbidden insight, a divine nudge?
Perhaps it is a time to reinvent ourselves
and become new again.

I believe it is a time
to leave the lost behind,
to work like life may never end,
to open doorways,
to leave your soul unlocked,
to welcome what is unexpected,
to pray like you never prayed before,
to wait, listen and hope.
Let tomorrow come.

Thanksgiving 2021

Today is Thanksgiving Day.
It is a time to say thanks
for all we have received
from our generous Earth—
food, family, friendship, faith
and so much more.

On this day,
we give great thanks
for all creatures, great and small,
with whom we share this land—
Shelly, Max, Jake,
Kit-Kat and Kitty.

Today we also remember and regret
the broken stories of our past,
stories of prejudice and pain,
of how our Indigenous sisters and brothers
were treated with violence and disdain,
robbed of faith, culture, land and respect,
their dignity denied.

On this day, we pray,
remember and give thanks
to those loved ones
who've gone before us
and those for whom we are grateful.

We also remember and give thanks
for all that has been and is yet to be.

We give thanks for each of us
gathered around the table
to participate in this Thanksgiving feast.

We also remember the prophetic voice
of Meister Eckhart,
whose words remind us
of the focus of this day:
"If the only prayer you ever say
in your entire life is thank you,
that will be enough."

Let's Pray

Thomas Merton taught me
something I hold close today.
If you think you cannot pray,
then pray as if you can.
Say amen
and let's pray for each other
on this sacred day.

Thanksgiving Prayer

We gather this day, surrounded by the beauty of Earth.

We awake to the wonder of this sacred gathering, enhanced by the magnificent stories that bind us together.

Today we welcome the pilgrim people: Joe, Erin, Patrick...

We celebrate within each moment the harmony, balance, and peace of the universe, as we breathe in and breathe out the spirit of the cosmos and the vitality of each life.

Christmas Prayer

We gather this morning, grateful and blessed by the wisdom and the beauty of the Christmas cactus.

At this precious moment, we gaze upon the paintings around the altar, each an expression of the cosmos and the soul. We are awash in the wonder of our unfolding journey.

We remember the birth of God's creation.

We wonder at the grace of beauty that cleanses and heals the hunger in each soul, as we honor the trees, which are the lungs of Earth, bringing forth energy and new life.

Family Prayer

How often have you heard it said
blood is thicker than water?
Never was that more true
than in Anita's family.
The bonds of love,
respect and gratitude
are wonderfully present
as the Braganza family
journeyed from Toronto
to Springbank for the Christmas season,
for wonderful moments
of stories, friendship and food.

Prayer of the Cosmos

ALL: The divine presence permeates all life. Each flower, child, cloud signifies the sacredness of all.

R: We gather as a people called forth by trust, promise, and compassion. Standing on the shoulders of those who have gone before, we remember our origins and the company of the mystics and prophets who join us on this journey.

We remember and give thanks to the originating energy of the universe, to the ancient One whose vast generosity brought us into existence and calls us forth today.

L: We remember and celebrate the great narrative of the universe, which reveals the depths of the past and the promise of the future and announces with clarity and hope a profound epiphany at this incarnational moment.

We gather as a holy people, called forth into circles of gratitude and of trust. We remember the scriptures of creation; those proclamations of divinity are inscribed in the sacred rocks on whose foundation our planet stands.

R: The shimmering beauty of the trees and flowers is an exaltation of existence, which shines forth in verdant wonder, as rainbows of sacredness manifest everywhere in our midst.

We celebrate also our companions on the way, our cousins of creation, who swim in the oceans, dance in the meadows, and soar above us in the sky.

L: We make our Eucharist today, embraced by the members of humanity who, with conscious self-awareness, illuminate our paths and show us the way.

R: We honor Jesus of the cosmos and Earth, who lived among us then and who now permeates, illuminates, and makes sacred every moment and molecule of existence.

L: We think also of the great cultural workers of yesterday and today, by whose lives we are inspired and who incarnate wisdom for this sacred, defining moment. We recall the mystics of the past and present: Meister Eckhart, Hildegard of Bingen, Teresa of Avila, John of the Cross, Julian of Norwich, Francis of Assisi, Clare of Assisi, Mechthild of Magdeburg, and so many more.

R: Among the prophets of yesterday and today are Gandhi, Pope John XXIII, Pope Francis, Dorothy Day, Teresa of Calcutta, Thomas Merton, Brother David Steindl-Rast, Pierre Teilhard de Chardin, Dr. Martin Luther King, Jr., Oscar Romero, Elizabeth Johnson, Ilia Delio, Barbara Fiand, Diarmuid O'Murchu, Leonardo Boff, Gregory Baum, Jack Egan, and the many saints and martyrs anonymously inscribed in the prophetic book of life.

L: We include the Earth saints from the present and the past who have reminded us to honor and care for our sacred home. Numbered among those who have taught us to be open to the primary revelation of creation, and whose existence has inspired literacy for life: Pope Francis, Rachel Carson, Thomas Berry, Jane Goodall, Kateri Tekakwitha,

Black Elk, Miriam MacGillis, Brian Swimme, Greta Thunberg, and others.

R: Mindful of brokenness and beauty all around, we now recall and gather to make our Earth an altar and to give thanks for all that was and is to be. Conscious of the sacredness of existence—that all is holy and infused with the divine Spirit—we take these simple elements of bread and wine, offspring of Earth, as a sign of each and the communion of all.

ALL: Inspired by the words inscribed in our tradition and announced by Jesus of the cosmos and cross, we remember and say, "This is my body."

Also inspired and nourished by the blood of Earth, which irrigates our souls and activates all life, we echo and recall the words of the last supper, and together we say, "This is my blood."

Together we proclaim our trust: I believe in the great Paschal moments of the universe, manifest in the galaxies and personified in the Cosmic Christ. I believe in the incarnational energy of the flaring forth, in the cosmic crucifixion of galaxies and stars. I believe in self-transcendence and new life, embodied and expressed in the emergence of Earth, life, and humans. I believe in Jesus of Nazareth and in his journey from the manger of Bethlehem, transfiguration on Mount Tabor, the cross of Gethsemane, the risen mystery of the empty tomb, and beyond. I believe in the enveloping mystery of the Cosmic Christ, whose hidden presence, manifest in every sight and sound, announces beauty, wonder, and belonging everywhere.

L: From our planetary altar, we behold a cosmos and a world alive with divine creative energy, pulsating, transfigured, and transformed every day in every way. Nourished for the journey, we take up our planetary task, embraced by the sacred envelope of life.

ALL: Empowered by the universe, we join our words and work with the great cosmic thrust that invites us into a future as yet unknown.

As new people, transfigured and transformed, we join the great Eucharistic banquet at the dawn of a new era, infused with cosmic wisdom. Grateful to the God of the cosmos, who invites us into partnership, we go forth to cocreate a new world, a new heaven, and a new Earth.

Whatever Needs to Be Done

Our lives are punctuated
by moments of wisdom,
gratitude and anticipation.

May each manifestation
bring wisdom and a listening heart
to whatever needs to be done.

With this in mind,
we venture forth
into the uncertain future.

While remaining hopeful,
we open ourselves
to the as-yet-unknown.

We venture forth and await
the unexpected as it washes
over the vast panorama of what is needed.

We listen deeply
with the ear of our heart,
preparing to take up the task before us.

The Exultet for Today's World: Easter Vigil 2021

It's Easter again! This night, with grateful hearts, we pray and give thanks for all who have joined us on this journey, both yesterday and today. Among them are Sisters Ursula and Karla, who with Trina engaged in an adventurous spark, and without any extraordinary power, set out to this sacred place of Springbank to reconstitute the Earth.

Tonight is a different time. It is a time of beauty and brokenness. On this holy night, we arrive at a deep, sacred moment in human-Earth history. We pray tonight for a time of inclusion, compassion, and peace. We give voice to the wonderful inclusive hymn "Red and yellow, black and white, we are all precious in God's sight." May this prayer flow across the hills of Georgia to China and the rest of the world.

In a world torn apart with prejudice and pain, may we once again listen and give great thanks as we proclaim and listen to the cry of the poor and the cry of Earth.

On this holy night, when our world is torn and tattered by racial injustice, may we once again listen to the words of Dr. Martin Luther King, Jr., who proclaimed, "I have a dream that my four little children will one day live in a nation where they will not be judged by the color of their skin but by the content of their character."

We once again listen deeply tonight and pray with hopeful supplication for a new time in human-Earth history, when all people of good will and all the creatures of creation will rise up in the springtime of this day, empowered in our souls by the greening power of hope.

We give great thanks today that we have arrived at this hope-filled moment, when we will be healed of the virus through vaccinations, when we will return to caring for the planet by realigning ourselves with the Paris Accord. May this be a time when once again our hearts and minds are hopeful and restored.

We venture forth to engage, that we may live in a time of clear water, in a healthy land, in a country where democracy has been restored and those who seek a safe home feel welcomed, when democracy will no longer be ruled by ballot box surprises and the will of all people will be restored.

Today we join with enthusiastic embrace to welcome a new era of hope, when we will once again join our hearts and hands in the fulfillment of our vocational destiny, empowered by each of our unique callings and gifts. May we join with sisters and brothers around the globe to create a more mutually enhancing world.

With gratitude and grace, we celebrate tonight the story of creation, liberation, and us. In blessing and brokenness, we experience a restoration of newness, rising from the wellsprings of our cultural soul. With wonder and surprise, we once again rediscover hope and recognize the imprint of the signature of God on every landscape, tree, and creature on our sacred Earth.

We feel the upsurge of grace and gratitude in our hearts as we celebrate on this Easter vigil night a new time, a new moment of grace that floods our awareness, activates our imagination, and embraces our souls.

On this holy night, we light the Paschal candle from the eternal fire of the great flaring forth. We announce once again the birth of our Easter journey as we remember and celebrate together that sacred moment when the universe and each of us were born.

Enveloped in the verdant moment of this South Carolina spring night, we celebrate our common journey in the memories of those who preceded us on the way. May this Paschal journey empower each of us as we listen deeply and make our Easter with Earth.

Jim Conlon

Solitude and Dark

Like a firefly dancing in the night,
peer into silence.

Solitude hovers in the dark,
on the no-longer-distant shore.

Let yourself be swept into mystery.
Hear the call that is fresh and unfolding.

Conscious Fear, Unconscious Wish

There are times in all our lives
when we prayerfully call out to the divine
with a deep longing in our soul.

In these sacred times,
we long for fulfillment,
while at the same time,
at some deeper level,
we oppose the very thing
for which we wish.

May we today
let fear dissolve into the fulfillment
of what we truly pray for.

Jim Conlon

Where Were You on 9/11?

Remember thirty years ago
on that 9/11 day
when you were on your way to the Y,
listening to the news.

Suddenly another voice announced
devastating news.
Planes crashed into the World Trade Center,
the Pentagon and the fields of Pennsylvania.

Where are you now?
Do you hear Saint Francis say,
"Make me an instrument of peace?"
To this question we all answer, "I do."

Death

Death is mysterious. It knows part of all our lives. When we die, life is changed, not ended. The dark night of our soul will inevitably culminate in morning.

Every experience reminds us that all of life is woven into a dance of death and rebirth. Life, death, resurrection. Our challenge—when we look back and peer into the mysteries of life—is to embrace the realization that without death, there can be no resurrection.

Jim Conlon

Descent

What do you say
when the days unravel,
when logic and focus
vanish into the far-off sky?

In the silence, I hear a cry
to all who dare to listen
with their heart,
to wander forth
onto uncertain paths.

Out of the darkness
dawn descends,
hope bubbles up
from the heart of wisdom.

The Other Side

The storm blew across the sea.
Today I call out,
"Please lead me to the other side."
There, the land is fertile,
the wind is calm.
The breeze is soft,
silent and deep.
Let me cross over
to the silent side,
where solitude sleeps
and grateful hearts abide.

Jim Conlon

How Do You Pray?

It was a late December afternoon in Derry, New Hampshire, during the Christmas holiday. A friend of my brother asked a penetrating question: "What is your spiritual practice?" In other words, "How do you pray?"

At first I felt startled and at a loss for a response. It was as if no one had asked me that question before, and I was unable and unprepared to respond.

Over the remaining days in New Hampshire, the question remained with me, awaiting a response.

To this day, this is my answer to the question that continues to live in my soul: I walk, I read, I write.

I walk:

To walk is to take in the beauty of creation: to feel the gentle breeze, to survey the flowers, and to greet the people and pets I meet.

During such walks, thoughts and feelings bubble up and come into consciousness. Perhaps questions hitherto left unasked now yield answers. For the most part, the walk is a time to read the book of nature and allow the images and sounds of the natural world to speak their wordless wisdom of beauty, touch, and taste. And smell. Here, the God we may not know becomes present in the sights and sounds of each stride and moment.

Each day, I rise from the resting of the night, ponder my dreams, the events of the day, and questions that remain unanswered in my awareness. Deep in my heart, I wish to live into the questions that remain as yet unanswered.

I read:

When I read, I pick up books from theologians, cosmologists, and spiritual writers who in their works and wisdom make significant connections between my lived experience and the eternal truths of my tradition. The writings of Teilhard de Chardin, Thomas Merton, and Thomas Berry are of particular significance. Others include Elizabeth Johnson, Rosemary Radford Reuther, Leonardo Boff, Judy Cannato, Diarmuid O'Murchu, Kathleen Deignan, and many more.

However, in my reading, I am also challenged to read the signs of the times and meditate on the hopes and dreams, challenges, and transformative work of people who live at this time or in the past. Culture has its wisdom to tell and its challenges to present, as do our hearts.

I am reminded of the time when I was a seminarian with Bob Keller at Sacred Heart Church in Saginaw, Michigan. Someone asked why he read the newspaper every morning. His response was, "I want to see what God is up to today."

I write:

When I write, I strive to make sense of my life, to create hopefully an integration between what I observe in my intrapsychic world and the world around me. I also seek to make shareable what I understand from the world around me.

As time allows each day, I express the conclusions and insights that surface from this awareness. With greater clarity and vision, I find an appropriate response to the questions that remain.

Earth

Silken sunshine
flows across my soul.
A day of wonder
heals each longing heart.
Witness the spring of life
gurgle forth
from the sacred emptiness
of our generous Earth.

Plans

Springbank stories bubble up today
from memories both vast and small
to irrigate each person's grateful soul.

The way ahead seems clearer now,
as with hearts and hands together,
we compose chapters yet untold.

Our Great Work

Each of us, on our journey, experiences the joy and sorrow of everything. Through this, our divine awareness is enhanced. As we reflect on our lives, we feel moved to ask:
- Who am I?
- Why am I here?
- What is my great work?

Today, in our time, we could say that our task is to move modern industrial civilization from its present extractive mode on Earth to a more benign, loving presence.

Since the terrorist attack of 9/11, we have entered a new era of anxiety. At this time, we witness the eroding influences of the great patriarchies of today; we witness financial organizations, the justice system, and religion eroding to the point where they seem to oppose their original purpose.

Thus, in and through our great work, we eagerly take up the task to create a world that is compassionate, sensitive, and generous.

Women's Wisdom

For half a millennium, First Nations women have been at the forefront of Indigenous peoples' resistance to cultural assimilation. Today they are still fighting for the survival of their cultures and their peoples—in the rain forest and the city, in the courts and legislatures, in the longhouse and the media.

The 1994 documentary *Keepers of the Fire* profiled Canada's Indigenous women who protected and defended their land, their culture, and their people in the time-honored tradition of their foremothers.

As women take their authentic place in society, the shadow side of the male-dominated church and society is exposed. With time, women are rising in society to be prophetic voices for equality and the culture of peace. Some notable names from the past are Madame Marie Curie for medicine, Maria Montessori for education, Rachel Carson for biology, and Barbara McClintock in genetic research. Women's wisdom also has been shared with the world by mystics such as Hildegard of Bingen, Teresa of Avila, and Julian of Norwich.

In our country today, we hear voices such as Kamala Harris, Deb Haaland (the first Native American woman holding the position of a cabinet minister), and the powerful poetic voice of young Amanda Gorman.

You may wonder what the world would be like if Hillary Rodham Clinton had become president in 2016.

Sacred Water

Today we once again embark on a reflective journey, as we imagine that each of these small vessels contains the sacred water of our childhood.

As we pour water into the larger bowl, we remember and give great thanks for the water that we were first surrounded by in our mother's womb, and the waters that surrounded us in our childhood years and beyond.

In the ceremony today, we share with each other our memories of the waters of our life, giving great thanks for the waters that unite us all and the Earth.

Unfinished

As we move forward in life,
we focus on the divine presence
that floods our awareness
with fresh realization.
The God of the universe
embraces each vital moment
of the cosmic web.
We become deeply aware
that the entire universe,
the cosmos and all that is
remain unfinished,
even as the sacred presence
continues to overflow
into each moment.

Our Broken Story

When science appeared to overwhelm the traditions of philosophy and theology, the sacred story of humanity was broken.

As we consider our story, we realize the impact of this breakage on our world and our psyche.

When our tradition is reduced to static dogma and our story is diminished, and when science is not yet understood as a true sacred story, we become lost. We are disconnected from the past and lack a sense of the future.

How the Scientific Story Becomes a Sacred Story

We live in a new era, the time of a new cosmology. Here at Springbank, we are engaged in creating a contemporary vision of our spiritual journeys, one that is a new chapter in the process of the great work, an evolutionary worldview that challenges and reinvigorates our spirituality.

Thomas Berry said we have arrived at the terminal stage of the cenozoic era, which was an era of beauty, flowers, diversity, and radiant energy. His prophetic vision reminds us that we are now in a technocratic era—an era of distance, mechanization, specialized expertise, and loss of fresh energy.

He spoke about the ecozoic era, a term he developed to give the believing community a vision and a sense of hope for a time when humans and the Earth will blossom forth to create a mutually enhancing culture.

With this vision in mind, we are able to become people of the ecozoic era and to celebrate a new sacred story that will include all our stories. Each of us is a paragraph in this great cosmological vision. It is a time for evolutionary faith, a time to shift from cosmos to cosmo-genesis, a time to embrace a fresh vision for the story and a new dream to engage each of us.

It is also a time to avoid two tendencies. One is that, because of our uncertainty and unclarity, we may be tempted to return to a fundamentalist, reactionary spiritual practice. The other tendency to avoid is the notion of some call a "new age," in which fear prompts us to abandon the core principles of our tradition.

Instead, let us become instruments and visionaries for a great transition into a long-awaited Paschal mystery—a new ecozoic era, manifesting as a living cosmology that does not forsake our traditional stories.

Sacred Heart Church in Port Lambton, 2017

I join you this morning in the town in which I was born, in the church where I was baptized. I join you today with gratitude as my brother and his four offspring—Chuck, Doug, Teresa, and Maria—join us this day.

Recently I visited St. Mary's Center. This model program serves the hungry and the unhoused in West Oakland, California.

On that day, I participated in a memorial service of gratitude as clients and staff gathered to give thanks and remember those who had gone ahead into eternal life. Each person was named, and a painted rock was placed in a memorial garden at the place where they had been sheltered, fed, and treated with dignity.

We give thanks and honor the names of our parents, grandparents, and siblings as we approach the Eucharist this morning.

My father, Richard, loved stories. In the evening, he would relax on our front porch and call out neighbors and friends alike: "Come up the steps and tell me a story."

Today we gather to remember and celebrate our story. We celebrate the stories, images, and memories through which we recall our origins.

We recall stories inscribed on cemetery markers, in baptismal records, and given to us by our ancestors. We remember our ancestors and give thanks for this moment.

I recall with gratitude those times when snow first carpeted the land in winter. And when the area was flooded with leaves of golden orange and red on fall and summer days. And when the stately St. Clair River glistened with beauty as we swam, fished, and sailed on her crystal waters.

As we drive across the landscape of Sombra and Port Lambton these days, we remember our ancestors who ventured forth from Ireland and France to settle and build the houses that today we call home.

As we remember our stories today, my mind goes back to memories of my first communion. In one picture, I stood with Fr. Dean and my classmates. Another picture I treasure is with our pastor, Fr. McMahon. In it, my brother Bob and I gathered with many others as the altar boys of Sacred Heart Port Lambton and St. John's Sombra.

This morning, I also recall that on May 31, 1964, I was privileged to celebrate my first mass at St. John's Sombra. That was fifty-three years ago. It is indeed a privilege to come home today and give thanks to this sacred place, which holds many memories for my brother and his children.

I remembered the schools in Sombra and Wallaceburg, as well as the baseball diamonds and skating rinks that were in many ways our classrooms for life.

I want to thank Frs. Gillespie and Bedard for their warm welcome and hospitality.

As we approach the altar this morning to celebrate the Eucharist, I echo the words of the prophet Dag Hammarskjold: "For all that has been, thanks. For all that will be, yes."

On this transfiguration Sunday, we remember the moment when Jesus was transfigured before his people as his garments became white as snow. This day, we ask, "What events have transformed and transfigured our lives?"

Among them, we count the mountain-top experience of civil rights leader Dr. Martin Luther King, Jr., in 1968, and his speech five years before that, when he described his dream of a world where little black children and little white children could be judged by the content of their character rather than the color of their skin.

For my brother and me, Sombra and Port Lambton have been our mountain-top experiences.

John O'Donohue says, "The human journey is a continuous act of transfiguration."

My prayer for each of you is that the divine spark will continue to shine and radiate in your lives, as you come to embody more and more the eternal diamond that is your true self.

Today I look back over the often-turbulent times of the last decades, punctuated by the Vietnam War, the civil rights movements, the political unrest in Canada and the USA, the transformative moment Pentecostal moment of Vatican II, and the inspiring leadership of Pope Francis. During these years, I engaged in parish ministry in Blessed Sacrament in London, Our Lady of Mercy in Sarnia, and St. Ursula in Chatham.

At this terminal phase of my life in ministry, I come home to Sacred Heart Church in Port Lambton with gratitude in my soul. I join each of you around the altar this morning and give great thanks for the gift to all of us, the gift of life.

Jim Conlon

Better Than the Past

There is so much to be thankful for.
Like stories of the storm last night,
when the fields became radiant with snow.

The night passed without damage or destruction.
Together we greet the morning, frosty and firm,
and shiver in astonishment at this new day.

May this cold winter morning bring us forward,
as once again we celebrate and proclaim
that tomorrow can be better than all the past.

The Challenge Before Us Now

Today, along with people such as Franciscan sister Ilia Delio, Teilhard de Chardin, Thomas Berry, Brian Thomas Swimme, and others, we are on the cusp of a new era. It is a time that calls us to participate and engage in the development of a more mutually enhancing universe.

Our journey is an unfolding, an adventure, a blossoming.

This new story is the manifestation of a profound, integral, creative, and zestful moment. It is a place to practice our listening heart, to give birth to the fresh expectations that are waiting to flourish forth in our midst.

The spirituality that is most alive today is based on an integration of our inherited tradition and an evolutionary worldview. Our challenge is to infuse this emerging spirituality into every aspect of life.

We understand that this challenge can be articulated in many ways. For example, we can speak of it as a fresh sense of the sacred, or as what Dr. Martin Luther King, Jr. called "the fierce urgency of now." Whatever way we express it, we can say with certitude that the future is no longer open ended, postponement is not the answer, and a collective response is called for.

Jim Conlon

Birth of a New Soul

Today we stand at the portals of a new civilization. We search for a vision that can carry us into fresh, transformative times. We strive to name the vision that is emerging from the creative outpouring of this new civilization, which is not yet but is about to be born.

As we reflect on what needs to be done, we acknowledge the need to breathe new life into the culture, to be open to the journey of letting go and of awakening to a new soul.

Seeking a vision that will energize more fully the potential and possibility of our lives, we gather in non-hierarchical communities, where we can share information, support, and common action.

Yet we seek more than the mere orchestration of beauty, diversity, and unity; we seek a vision and focus for a society in search of its very soul.

This new soul will show up in the healthy interdependence of interconnected circles. It comes to us as a life-sustaining arc that is the continuation of the original fire ball.

As we awaken to the transforming energy of our dreams for a global civilization, may the articulation of this vision assist us in building a cosmic community that gives it full expression.

Together, we proclaim the vision of a healthy planet where we shall remove all poison from the air, we shall cease all pollution of the water, we will cease all contamination of the Earth, we shall be open to the life-giving radiance of the sun, and we shall support the self-sustaining forces of the universe.

Jim Conlon

Each Day

Each day, here on this planetary altar,
I celebrate wonder and give thanks,
that we together are alive
and profoundly aware of the need
for a wellspring of compassion
in each moment of our lives.

Birth awakens at each moment
as we continue to await
the hour of the unexpected
rolling out before us.
New life is ever-expanding into
a vast surge of blessing and light.

Together we illuminate the darkness,
make all things never forgotten,
erupting into a sea of fresh possibilities,
offering a cosmic promise
to illuminate and transcend the world,
here on the precipice of new beginnings.

Matthew Fox: Early Years

Matthew (Timothy) was born in 1940 in Madison, Wisconsin, the son of a Catholic father and a Jewish mother. Timothy loved sports and was encouraged by his father, who was a football coach for the University of Wisconsin.

As a young person, Timothy was afflicted with polio. For some time, there was a question as to whether he would lose his ability to walk. Thankfully, that was not the case.

As a young man, Timothy was attracted to devotion for the Blessed Mother. He often attended the Saturday liturgy, which was focused on Mary.

Early in life, Timothy entered the Dominican order in the central province of the United States. He was ordained as Matthew.

During his early academic work, it was clear that Matthew was gifted and that doctoral work would follow. He was uncertain about where to go to study, so he wrote to Thomas Merton for advice. Matthew's book *A Way to God*, about Merton, includes that correspondence.

Following Merton's advice, Matthew enrolled in a doctoral program in the École Biblique in Paris.

There, he met Father Marie-Dominique Chenu OP. Fr. Chenu was a popular author and well known for his writings and participation in the vision of the second Vatican Council.

Matthew Fox and Fr. Chenu

It was Monday morning in 1990. Some students and Matthew Fox were gathered in the chapel of Holy Names University for prayer. The leader was Neal Douglas-Klotz, author of several books, including *Prayers of the Cosmos* and *Desert Wisdom*.

When the prayer time came to an end, Matthew spoke to us. He said, "Today I learned that Father Chenu, who was my mentor and guide during my doctoral work, has passed away."

In the days that followed, Matthew revealed his deep gratitude for Fr. Chenu's role in his life. Among the many gifts that Chenu provided was the term *creation spirituality*, which came to define Matthew's work.

Fr. Chenu left a powerful imprint on Matthew in many ways. Matthew went on to write many popular books that have had a significant impact on the spiritual practice of the American church. His thesis was self-published in 1971 as *Religion USA: Religion and Culture by Way of Time Magazine*.

I find it mysterious that Mepkin Abbey is also associated with *Time Magazine*. The family of Claire Booth Luce, who were publishers of *Time* and other magazines, also endowed the abbey.

The first time I met Matthew was in the summer of 1983, at York University.

I later understood through my participation in the Institute in Culture and Spirituality (ICCS) at Holy Names University how the program Matthew had created was in many ways an expression of what he learned in France from Fr. Chenu.

Matthew Fox: Creation Spirituality

Matthew's book *Original Blessing*, published in 1983, became a bestseller. It sparked a fresh and revitalized progressive moment in the American church.

Speaking of creation spirituality, Matthew said, "To recover a spiritual tradition in which creation and the study of creation matters would be to inaugurate new possibilities between spirituality and science that would shape the paradigms for culture, its institutions, and its people."

The golden years of this work, from 1984 through 1996, were marked by the popularity of *Original Blessing* and subsequent books by Matthew, including *The Coming of the Cosmic Christ, Creation Spirituality*, and various books about Christian mystics.

Matthew's work became the catalyst for an emerging movement. He travelled internationally and had a growing influence on the American church. I was privileged to work with him during those years.

I worked with Matthew to develop a program called Regional Connectors. Through it, people from around the country, Canada, and beyond were provided with information and support and the possibility for common action. As Matthew's work became more international, the influence of creation spirituality continued to expand and grow.

During my thirteen years of working with Matthew, I became aware that ICCS was a program of engaged spirituality.

One of the most significant contributions of Matthew's work was his departure from the classical spiritual paradigm of purgation, illumination, and union. Instead, he developed a new articulation of the spiritual journey that he called *The Four Paths.*

Don't Shrink

Don't shrink from the challenge.
Give thanks for this moment.
Embrace what is next.
With gratitude, give thanks
that somewhere within
the seemingly dormant dust of the past,
rains a profound parable
that savors and nourishes life.
Its ever-active imprint on my soul
has created an enduring impulse
that makes possible
the expanding manifestation
of goodness, wisdom and truth.

The Four Paths: *Via Positiva*

The *via positiva* is characterized by the befriending of creation, by incarnation. It is about joy, delight, and pleasure.

On this path, the seeker awakens to a realized eschatology.

The wisdom of panentheism, where God is present in all things and all things in God, removes all dualism.

We begin to experience a sacred presence overflowing into all things. We develop an enhanced ecological sensitivity that can lead us to an ecological approach, toward caring for the planet.

It was on this path that, although distinct, Matthew Fox's vision coincided with that of Thomas Berry.

The Four Paths: *Via Negativa*

The *via negativa* is characterized by letting go and letting be. It is about embracing darkness, letting go of images, sinking into emptiness.

Matthew's articulation of the *via negativa* is my personal favorite of his writings. The focus on letting go and letting be can be related to the writings of Meister Eckhart, who said, "Isness is God" and who thus urged us to let go and let be.

For example, when my brother began to come to terms with his diagnosis of Parkinson's disease, he said, "I guess it's my time to let go."

When we let go, we surrender our power and we allow images, thoughts, and feelings to simply pass through our consciousness.

It's like looking at a fish bowl. A little fish comes along, stops at the glass for a moment, and then moves on. In other words, images come into our mind, we notice them, and we let them go. This is the practice of the *via negativa*, which is perhaps the most profound dimension of creation spirituality.

The practice of letting go and letting be is a vast liberation event. It is dialectical and deep. When we are truly able to let go, then out of nothingness, we also allow God to be God.

It is an act of the imagination whereby we let go of all that holds us back in life. In the recesses of our soul, holy mystery becomes the abiding act of our imagination.

Out of our interior emptiness, it becomes possible for divinity to flow into us. It is through our experience of emptiness and our openness to nothingness that the divine flows into our heart, mind, and soul.

Jim Conlon

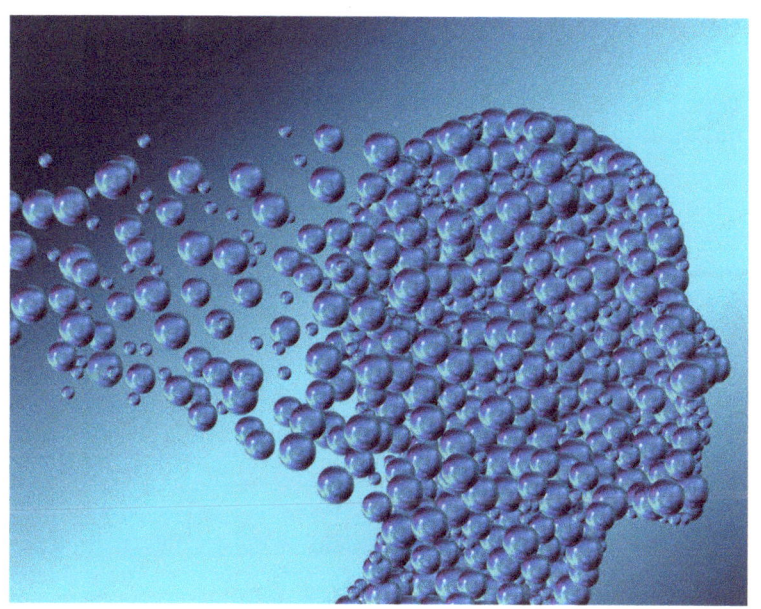

Our Vision Realized

We cross the threshold
into a new planetary civilization,
where beauty shines forth
as our story continues to unfold
in an always yet-unfinished world.

We realize not only
the goals and purposes
of the global civilization,
but the strategies and actions
necessary to accomplish them.

Through each new image,
metaphor and art work,
we move forward
to fulfill the planet and ourselves,
to continually co-create the beauty
we are called upon to ponder and pursue.

As the global civilization comes into focus,
the whole world becomes a sacrament:
every blossom of clover,
every drop of rain,
every intuitive thought,
every song that tells of beauty,
every blade of grass,
every dandelion and spider's web,
every moment of wonder and mystery,
every greening impulse.

Next Teardrop

Perhaps now is the time
to dive deeply
into the increasing awareness
that it is still possible
to heal what is broken
and renew the face of the Earth.
With this in mind,
I look forward
to each new tomorrow
and await the next teardrop to fall.

The Four Paths: *Via Creativa*

The *via creativa* is characterized by creativity flowing from a deep experience of the divine energy.

After an experience of radical letting go in the *via negativa*, we give birth to something new, that it may become vital and vibrant in our life. With a fiery spirit, we transform the world.

One of the great challenges on the spiritual journey is expressed through the words "I can't." But creativity says, "Yes I can!"

Life does not ask what we believe as much as it asks what we will give birth to.

What we choose to give birth to in and through our imagination results in acts of creativity. For example, Thomas Merton was a photographer. Gandhi practiced the spinning wheel. Anita plays the piano.

The ultimate spiritual act is when we give birth to compassion. It is then that we can discover our identity through acts of creativity.

What flows out of us through creativity also remains within us. For example, a parent may raise a child into adulthood. But that child never leaves the parent's heart.

It is sometimes said that God is the youngest among us. This is because creativity is always present in each new moment. When seen through divine eyes, everything is always brand new.

Unfortunately we have separated creativity from religion. However, Doreen's dance in the liturgy was itself a creative act.

Jim Conlon

Creativity

Creativity is the nexus
from which our vision
for a new civilization is born.
We are called today
to create a fresh and vibrant beauty
that was not here before.
Our challenge,
which is also our gift,
is to plunge courageously
into deep wells of wisdom,
to realize the creative energy
of the divine bubbling up
and pulsating through
every molecule and person
on this sacred Earth.

The Four Paths: *Via Transformativa*

The *via transformativa* explores the expression of what is free of suffering, what is just, and what is compassionate.

Jesus's words "Be perfect as your Heavenly Father is perfect" are often misunderstood. A more correct interpretation is "Be compassionate as your Heavenly Father is compassionate."

Meister Eckhart said, "The only way to live is like the rose, which lives without a why." In other words, to live in a world of justice, we are challenged to overcome our tendency to engage in abstractions.

It is also true that unless creativity is critiqued by the *via transformativa*, it can have negative results.

For example, I was sitting next to a man on an airplane who was a scientist. I asked him what he did. His answer came back that he was one of the scientists who developed a projectile that can either heal or cause destruction. It could do both. Therefore, the *via transformativa* is needed so that our creativity can be guided by compassion and not by destruction.

The bishops of the world in 1971 declared that justice is basic to the Gospel. Nevertheless, justice has often been relegated to a sense of obligation. It has been viewed as a glum, plodding abstraction. And it has been used to induce guilt.

In recent years, I have begun to explore the notion that beauty is a compassionate expression for harmony, balance, and enduring peace.

We can also say that justice is a manifestation of cosmic integrity.

For most of my life, I have felt called to bring about a liberating possibility for those who are oppressed. Such acts of justice flow from passion, love, risk, and freedom. Justice thus becomes a means to be delivered to myself, to walk through life guided and empowered to be the person I am meant to be, and to invite others to do the same.

When I ponder what needs to be done, I reflect on the call to bring beauty to the world and contribute to the unfolding dynamics of the universe. I pray that my modest efforts will contribute to the well-being of people and all creation.

Only Now

To be big hearted, courageous,
willing and ready to engage,
encounter, probe and envision—
this is my purpose,
my invitation,
my call.

As the days unfold
and the unseen continues to reveal,
I remain engaged
in longing for what is yet to be.

What seemed a thousand miles
now only appears one inch.
Now, as if for the first time,
I feel united and in tune with the infinite.

Jim Conlon

Questions

What is there left to do
but look back at your life,
and then look forward?
Ask the big question:
"What awaits me,
what remains to be done?"
Consider what is greater:
the value of the past
or the promise in what lies next.

Imagine a World

Imagine a world where, as Thomas Merton says,
"Every non two-legged creature is a saint."

Imagine a world where, as Hildegard of Bingen says,
"The soul is not in the body; the body is in the soul."

Imagine a world in which, like Mechthild of Magdeburg,
We see "all things in God and God in all things."

Imagine a world where, as Thomas Berry says,
"The universe is communion of subjects,
not a collection of objects."

Imagine a world where, as Thich Nhat Hanh says,
We "hear within us the sound of the Earth crying."

Imagine a world where, as Pope Francis says,
We "integrate questions of justice in debates on the environment, so as to hear both the cry of the Earth and the cry of the poor."

Imagine a world where, as Jesus says,
"Blessed are those who hunger and thirst, for they shall see God," where we can "come away to a deserted place and rest awhile."

Getting Started

Gustavo Gutiérrez provides a planetary view in his book *We Drink from Our Own Wells*.

He challenges us to create a deeper way to follow Jesus. Liberation theology and creation theology extend the understanding of the anawim and the poor and the dispossessed. The poor are not only the two-legged, the poor also include the land, the water, the trees, the animals, and all expressions of creation that are without choice.

Compassion is the creation-centered invitation to commit ourselves to a dynamic integration of justice-making and joy.

By giving birth to a fresh social consciousness, we become energized to heal what is broken and to renew the face of Earth.

In and through this process, we are empowered to foster a transformation of consciousness and to create a community of interdependence and a culture of enduring hope.

Medieval mystic Meister Eckhart described ministry as the engagement in whatever needs to be done. This purpose envelops Springbank Retreat and all those who hunger for a creative vision and are awake to the new creation-centered civilization that is about to be born.

May this be a time of hope and transformation, in which trust is deepened and the path forward emerges from the deep wells of wisdom of our peoples and Earth.

Welcome

Land, trees, flowers,
even rocks along the way,
be here now, new friends.
Cast your tomorrows
on the waters of life.

Welcome sacred seekers,
trust each new tomorrow.
Listen and wait,
expect surprises,
even if they upset your plans.

The Radiance of Springbank

An old song resonates in my heart: "I believe for every drop of rain that falls, a flower grows."

I believe Springbank and her evolving spirit provide such a glorious and radiant energy to all who are able to listen and receive it.

With each passing day, I feel an enhanced flow of energy. It breathes a revitalizing life force into the future of every soul it encounters.

Springbank's story touches and extends to all that is sacred. Its program radiates acceptance and makes possible the flourishing of an energetic freshness.

Springbank is a sacred place that celebrates wisdom and listens to the pulse of the planet. Its radiance continues to overflow into a profound experience of aliveness, embracing every flower, animal, and person.

Jim Conlon

Epilogue: Concluding Prayer

Welcome the sunlight
as it dispels the shadows of the night.
Bring forth fresh wisdom for the greening of Earth.
Open your heart and mind to the not-yets of your day.
Dissolve past pain,
allow your false self to float away.
Savor this moment, contemplate now.
Put all undue urgency to rest,
embrace this moment with great thanks.
Amen.

About the Author

Jim Conlon was born in Canada in 1936. He received a degree in chemistry from Assumption University of Windsor, and later in theology from the University of Western Ontario, and a PhD from Union Institute and Graduate School. Deeply moved by the impact of the second Vatican Council, the civil rights movement, and the Vietnam War, Jim moved from pastoral work to the streets. He was the recipient of the 2013 Thomas Berry Award. Today he is one of the leading teachers of the new narrative of the cosmos.

For more information and a complete list of Jim's published works, see: www.jimconlon.net.

Contact: Springbank: 843-372-6311 or springbank@springbankretreat.org

www.ingramcontent.com/pod-product-compliance
Lightning Source LLC
Chambersburg PA
CBHW040420100526
44589CB00021B/2773